This Book Belongs To

....

Made in the USA
Las Vegas, NV
12 September 2023

77362774R00070